£1.50

Horses Between Our Legs

Patricia McCarthy

Patricia McCarthy

AGENDA EDITIONS

ISBN 978-1-908527-18-9

First published 2014
Reprinted 2015

Agenda Editions
The Wheelwrights
Fletching Street
Mayfield
East Sussex
TN20 6TL

Design and production by JAC design
Crowborough, East Sussex

Printed and bound in Great Britain by
TJ International Ltd, Padstow, Cornwall

In honour of my two grandfathers (whom I never knew), my father and his three brothers who all served in The Great War, and of my mother who was a little girl then.

And in loving memory of my own little horse, Polka Necta, July 1, 1982 – May 5, 2014.

Biography

Patricia McCarthy, winner of The Poetry Society's National Poetry Competition 2013, is the editor of the national/international poetry journal, *Agenda*. She is half Irish and half English. After Trinity College, Dublin, she lived in Washington D.C., Paris, Bangladesh, Nepal and Mexico. She has been settled for a long time in Mayfield, East Sussex. She was Head of English at St. Leonards Mayfield School. A small collection, *Survival*, was published in the US and *A Second Skin* came out from Peterloo Poets in 1985. A translation of Rainer Maria Rilke's *Book of Hours* was published in 2007, translated by both Patricia McCarthy and Christine McNeill. A substantial collection, *Rodin's Shadow* (Clutag Press/Agenda Editions) came out in October 2012. *Around the Mulberry Bush: New & Selected Poems* is due from Waterloo Press 2014. Her work has appeared in many journals and she has been widely anthologised. In 2012 she was elected a Fellow of the English Association.

Acknowledgements:

Thanks to the editors of the following in which some of these poems have appeared: *Poetry Review, The Irish Times, The London Magazine, Temenos, Long Poem Magazine, Scintilla, Poetry Ireland, Stand.* 'Virginia Woolf's Angels 1919' was *The Guardian's* chosen poem of the week. 'Clothes that escaped the Great War' won the Poetry Society's National Poetry Competition, 2013.

Many thanks also to Studland Village Hall for permission to use the painting, 'Lady of the Black Horse' by George James Rankin on the front cover of this poetry collection.

Contents

Front cover: The Lady of the Black Horse
(oil on canvas by George James Rankin, 1916)

Clothes that escaped the Great War

Not the familiar ghosts: the shaggy dog of Thorne Waste
that appeared only to children; the chains clanking
from the Gyme seat, nor the black barge at Waterside.

These were the most scary, my mother recalled: clothes
piled high on the wobbly cart, their wearers gone.
Overalls caked in dung, shirts torn from the muscle strain

of heavy hemp sacks, socks matted with cow-cake
from yards nearby, and the old horse plodding, on the nod.
Its uneven gait never varied whether coming from farms

where lads were collected like milk churns, or going back
with its harvest of dungarees scented by first fags,
notes in pockets to sweethearts; boots with laces undone,

jerseys knitted – purl, plain – around coke fires.
And the plod, plod, quadruple time; then the catch
in the plod from the clank of loose shoes, from windgalls

on the fetlocks of the horse, each missed beat on the lane
a missed beat in a heart. As a small girl she could see –
at their windows – the mothers pressing memories

too young for mothballs into lavender bags, staring out
propaganda posters, dreading the shouts of telegraph boys
from lines of defence and attack. As the harness creaked

and the faithful old horse clopped forward and back,
the lads were new-dressed in the years never to be had,
piled higher than high over the shafts of the buckling cart.

Evening Walk, 1918

Proud of her mission, she would run, she said, with her brother
over the dykes as if over lines of cross-fire, feet catching in coils
of eglantine. The moon hung above was a truant-inspector

and they'd race, faster than the whizz-bangs shaking the sky –
to the market square. There they'd queue with a florin, shoved
by elders they imagined were enemy soldiers, to buy

the *Evening Gazette*. Its print would rub off on their hands,
blurring the headlines that they needed to know, branding them
conspirators. Back they'd rush, past the rickety bandstand:

miniature messengers brandishing the shields of Bellerophon, Mars.
For three and a half miles, they'd leap rabbit-hole craters,
the newspaper a scroll of fate beneath an arm, nenuphars

white and yellow warning-lights in the sucking marsh. Home
again, they'd unpeel each page like an onion, layer by layer,
daring each other to go first in the dreadful game: to comb

the list of names, hawk eyes ready to pounce on any prey.
Could he be found, their tall, brave father, shrunk to a whalebone
on some foreign unpronounceable beach? Or had he gone astray,

nameless, in a killing field? How much longer could they hold him
as a catch in their breath, confirming him for one more day?
Would he appear again in windows accustomed to the dim –

when colours danced, and everyone began in concert to sing
Rule Britannia, handkerchiefs waved in the air, the town magnified:
a metropolis, even its mill-sirens wailing to *God save the King?*

Jumping with the flames in the bonfire, she and her brother were magi,
jugglers, clowns. And on the dykes, over lifelines no longer crossed,
eglantine briars strangled the Kaiser's charred effigy.

'A Mental Case'

i.m. Emily Davison 1913

i

A blue stocking, she had no knowledge
how horses, by their instinct, avoid

trampling on humans; at full gallop
round Tattenham Corner no chance to pull up

without ligaments, tendons torn,
stress fractures, over-reaches, broken down.

Silent the crowd. Swishing past, the horses
too fast for recognition on the course,

even the outsiders, without form, like Anmer.
Suddenly from behind a barrier her tiny figure

in front of him jumps. Heads crane, binoculars
shake. And a red, green, purple banner

flutters for the single second that horse, jockey
and woman flatten the ground. Is she crazy.

suicidal, a martyr? About to tread in divots,
the race presumed over? What of the tickets

found in her pocket for the return journey
to town, for that evening's suffragette soireée?

ii

Her track record: stone-thrower, arsonist,
Hunger-striker, jailbird: not known to desist

From violence when the Cause required,
Flinging herself down staircases if inspired.

Hidden in the crypt of a Parliament house,
For residence on a census, plenty of nous.

Grabbing horses by the bridle in Morpeth,
In practice for Derby Day, careless of death.

High-stepping hackneys in harness in the park
Would not stop for her to make her mark

Pinning to browbands a scarf like a rosette,
Plodding vanners and cobs a better bet.

Emily, Emmeline listened to, acted upon:
Women freed for service in World War One.

iii

King George visited one of the days
Left to her, four before she died.
The jockey too would have been by her side,
Had he not been dragged by the horse
recovering after the fall, his foot
Stirrup-caught. Haunted he was
And aged by her 'poor upturned face'
Flashing before him on the turf,
Until he, too, lost consciousness –
Only to recover, remember and to bless.
King George visited her in distress,
As she ducked, now, under the barrier
Of life, force-fed by Death. Flouting fear
She waved her flag as she passed from here.

*None of the King's horses, none of the King's men
Could put Emily Davison together again.*

Another War Horse

(a privately-owned horse about to be requisitioned for World War 1)

'...and I whispered to the horse: trust no man in whose eye you don't see
yourself reflected as an equal.' Don Vincenzo Giobbe, circa 1700

i

The Last Ride

I ride you, my little other half,
as if on the Day of Judgement maybe,
where summer is rolled into late stooks

and winter lurks, hoary, drenching
the ground with mists at which you spook.

The breeze, fly-ridden, whips the ferns
into gangrenous fingers of admonition
lest a delay in shady copses should lead

through powdered paths to procrastination.
The better going suggests speed

and we canter along, extended between
breath and season, you on a long rein,
in outline only: the wood's bay stain.

Who was it said we never should
play here? We leap the abyss of a sett

spiked by brambles that jab your sides
with spurs meant for me rather than you.
Lengthened shadows have climbed trees to hide

from autumns that bleed. Nothing is new
except our mutual trust as we slide down

a scree to an old pond bay where hurricanes
and hail slosh in a black treacle brew.
Then gallop off, past unregistered stallions

and wall-eyed trotters you do not pursue
out of a life-long loyalty to me

despite your herd instinct. Where mists part,
we reject easy divisions of good and bad flocks
on each side and continue into the heart

of experience – through docks
which calm stings from the horizon

lassooing you. In this world
of segregations in fur, feather, fold,
we steady each weald, each wold.

I never need take a hold.
Then we float off, a single streak

through war cries of vixens, pheasant cocks
practising you for worse. With your hocks
under you, we chase off fear

of the call-up, jumping stooks
away from where I will have to sacrifice you.

ii

The Last Groom

Your summer coat I brushed, stroking one way
the velour of its velvet so that my image
reflected there would brand itself onto you
and I would be your amulet on The Front

keeping you from drowning in slurries of mud,
from cannon bones snapped by shell holes,
from ligaments left on barbed wire spools.

My Polka, my Darcey, Bess of my dreams,
splotched by bullets that removed your sheen.

My fingers I wanted as your nose plugs
in mustard gas attacks, the imprint of my face
your gas mask to prevent you trashing it
like a feed bag as you grabbed mouthfuls of air.

One last time I combed your well-pulled mane,
plaiting into it my own brown hair, then breathed
slow, into your neck till you exhaled long breaths –

My Polka, my Darcey, Bess of my dreams,
splotched by bullets that removed your sheen –

in time to mine: a duet to fill your manger
when you'd be gone. Into the stable's corner
I pushed you gently, darkening you
into a shadow that no call-up would want.

I could not prevent the ghosts of herds gone
whickering wild for rescue through the slats,
fistulous withers, tendons bowed, racks

of ribs far too pronounced. As I picked out
your feet, oiled your hooves, I pretended
we were off to a show, beribboned, buffed.
But No. You had to be broken in – to War.

My Polka, my Darcey, Bess of my dreams
on livery in my heart, fit always for queens.

iii

The Requisition Yard

No prayers, no rituals for the break of bonds
between horse and man; just commands
like whips on the flanks of the horses lined up

for suitability by size, breed, colour. No choice
but to resign you to this mock parade-ground,
blurred by steam from the sweat and loose droppings

of terrified mounts, ears twitching forwards
and back, by some sixth sense seeing into
their stunted futures, tolerating pain. Just as well

I could not hear you whicker to me when I retreated,
as if stabbed in the back; nor watch your nostrils
flare wide at the inspection: a punch on a back,

pinches down a leg, flexion tests for soundness.
Better too that I could not catch your eyes weeping
from something other than flies, the flash

of their whites amid the buzzing as, with scissors
and knives, manes were hogged, tails docked,
uniforms disembodied in the gloom, irrespective

of rank. I could imagine panic spreading
like an infection through the ropes while splints
got fired, straw wisps banged, burnt rinds

of hooves scavenged by strays. I could not look back
and, in a slumped fraternity of private owners,
I bowed my head in premature bereavement.

What officer would have you, I wondered,
with racing winners in your blood, your light mouth
unspoilt by harsh hands. Would you halt four square

at a braced back, as I had schooled you, dance
laterally over mud as through grass, knackered, with colic
from the sand? In the distance the clatter up a ramp

I tried not to hear; then carriages on a rail shunted
through an engine's steam. I could do nothing but stare
at your hairs preserved in silent dandy brushes,

pull from my pocket a strand of your tail teased out
to sleep on under the tarpaulin of a merciless khaki sky.
I would have preferred you to die as I held you,

loved, safe in the munch of an apple, in the forehead
a bullet – rather than pray in vain to find your noble face
over the stable door. Not lost in the annals of war.

iv

Coming to Terms

Months I have not been able to look at the fields.
Your absence has stood there like a presence

in the most boggy corner, tethered to the rope
of my loss weathering slowly to a strand frayed

with the long scutch grass. Tonight there is
no moon, only snow squeaking like a mind

resisting amnesia, giving me its eerie light
to detect you sheltered by your favourite holly,

icicles serrating your mane. Your ears
are pricked, your white blaze an exclamation mark,

of delight, as always, at my approach. From tall clumps
ungrazed too long, I pick your hoofprints to hang

about my wrist. Your droppings that outlive you,
in a pile, have hardened into bullets of knackers

who will shoot again for expedience and not preserve
the copper radiance torn from your coat as you slump.

Best to let you graze in memory, myself your rubbing post,
as this expanse blots out boundaries, erases misdeeds.

Your long red mane sweeps the snow which blanches you
with its deeps, teaching us both to withstand extremes.

Horse Code

Enrolment of women in the First Aid Nursing Yeomanry in the Great War

*'And God took a handful of southerly wind, blew his breath upon it,
and created the horse'.* Bedouin legend

Horses between our legs, brains between our teeth,
we enrolled: ten shillings, five foot three tall at least,
age seventeen to thirty five; a sheath

of certificates in veterinary work: bandages, splints
amputations; home nursing – and first aid,
pomades swapped for swabs of iodine, lint.

Partnered by our own muscled well-schooled horses
wind-swift, first thrusters on the hunting field
over ditches, banks, fit for any force –

we took part, tack well oiled, uniforms cut
to paper patterns: hand-stitched scarlet tunics,
riding skirts navy, braid-edged, plumed hard hats.

From country seats, double barrel names,
we wanted to prove we could level-peg any man,
use morse code against warped war games.

Trampled into trenches, our egos and ranks, what
a cavalry we were, drilled in charging to rescue,
across our pommels, the wounded – over packets

of cordite, dud shells, wire, to rickety hospitals
swilling in blood. Our only promotion a demotion
in camouflage khaki, riding astride on saddles

that crippled our mounts, caused girth galls.
La-di-dah or not, we gave our all, camaraderie
our recompense. Chins up, corseted still, we sat tall.

The FANY ladies

Posh slut, easy lay, privileged tart:
shouts from the privates into pink faces,
their well-bred horses in shell-shock.

Lilian, Mabel, Phyllis, Grace:
brave founding women of an army
whose gender filled an urgent space:

wires for telephones laid in fields,
non-horsey soldiers taught how to sit
by balance, with giving hands,

reins like silk, no reliance on bits,
the horse's body a river in full flow,
legs in breeches the mossed banks of grit.

Brave founding women galloping by,
wrapped hooves soundless – Calais,
Ypres, Ghent – through falling glass

and masonry. Ragtime tunes play
with bombardments in their heads –
waggons of the wounded escorted each day

to barges, trains, hospitals of tents, sheds.
Lilian, Mabel, Phyllis, Grace –
in clouds of mosquitoes, tsetse flies,

Bengers Food on offer, whatever the place.
Of the *posh slut, easy lay, privileged tart,*
their medals and headstones bore no trace.

Recreation Song

Soligny-la-Trappe, March 1916

Singalongsingalongsingalongsing
That's what to the troops us girls bring

In recreation huts – cakes for comfort,
Cocoa, gramophone records to sort

From spikes in wood boxes. To melodeons,
Harmonicas, rented pianos, accordeons

Squeezed like lungs we *singalongsing*
Centimes, farthings, halfpennies, shillings

Rattle in tincans as we play bagatelle
Lads and officers, matrons and belles.

We dance to our choruses, kick up legs
Then tell fortunes from every cup's dregs.

Singalongsingalongsingalongsing
We try to stay human with this kind of fling

On nerves that quake, on nerves of steel
Pinned to survival's rickety wheel.

In recreation huts of bricks, corrugated iron,
Rags, dried manure, leathered skins –

English lessons, newspapers, magazines
We keep half sane in emergency canteens.

A FANY Woman on the Front

Who is it I flee from on the horse cast in gold
mindless of tripwires in the unseasonable cold?

As he speeds up, trampling on nuggets
of light filtered by the sun through trees,
I crouch low, measuring how sound he is, how bold.

We streak along, arrow-marks carved on boughs
creaking into his free rhythms while the wind soughs

through his headstrong loneliness and nobility.
On curved runners once carved for me, he rocks me.
Forever, it seems, we flee while impulsion allows,

communicating by touch, thought, from whoever
thunders up behind. This year, next, sometime, never…

My avatar, with nostrils flaring, light on his feet,
he takes miles in his stride until at earth's final verge
we halt, four square, before the horizon which severs

itself from the lines we must go beyond. We stand
a single ghost, in the threat he hears overland,

in the shrieks in his eyes from carrousels
on which skeletons ride with a rattle, settlements
sucked down into the quickest of quicksands.

Who is it I flee from on the horse cast in gold
mindless of tripwires in the unseasonable cold?

Ragtime Song

After Scott Joplin's 'Maple Leaf Rag'

And
                one and two three and four five
six and seven eight and nine ten
And the
                voiceboxes of the wounded
we tap like woodpeckers for songs
And then
                test how long they can hold
their breath – to the flip-flap of wings

The winner has sixtyfour notes in one go
                John McCormack his man.

And we
                harmonise with the whinnies
as vocal cords of chargers are cut –
And with
                updraughts of the winds
pigeons take – roucou –

as they home to coke fires around fenders,
                sweet pea screens, hollyhocks

And then
                one and two three and four five
six and seven eight and nine ten
So we
                get them all to let rip
bawl out their worries and pain

till the voiceboxes of the wounded
                rise above toads' cold-blooded croaks
                sonorous and lyrical again.

Song of the Munitionettes

Peggy, Gladys, Lilian, Mabel, Elsie, Pearl
Such dangerous work not expected of a girl

Blowing ourselves up in youth's sweet prime
Daredevils we were, borrowed on borrowed time.

We sang if our wheezes and gasps allowed
Blue from breathlessness: quite a crowd.

In turbans of headscarves we chainsmoked
On breaks for stewed tea. Then back to poke

Cordite into shells, from housework on leave –
Only seven-day repetitive shifts to achieve.

Peggy, Gladys, Lilian, Mabel, Elsie, Pearl
Ash-grey faces, scarlet lips of show girls

Cyanosis successful in its merciless tricks.
Unskilled martyrs, our slog not for kicks –

Brainwashed we were as suppliers of war
No wolfwhistle, pinched bum to restore

Fun with lads whose pinups we could have been.
Dangling on strings behind the scenes

We choked and spluttered in toxic fumes.
Little chance we ever had to bloom.

The washing strung over streets – for us girls
Remained the only flip-flap flags to unfurl.

Remount Depot

'The Kaiser's order expressing his desire that the
wives of German army officers shall immediately
discontinue the practice of riding astride is being very
widely and keenly discussed by horsewomen all over
the country. The fact that it comes so soon after
King George's refusal to witness any exhibition
of riding astride at Olympia is regarded as significant'.
The Times, March 17th, 1914

Our string of horses we trotted past villages
to whistles through teeth and shouts of *giddy up*
from butchers, bakers, candle-stick makers.

No thoroughbreds training for steeplechases –
these ribby old carthorses and cobs strode out,
blood up from bucketfuls of oats, chargers

recuperating from war, gentled by the softness
in our voices, some as shell-shocked as those
who fought from their backs. On we clattered –

fancied by farmhands who slapped their thighs
in stackyards at our approach, then stripped us
with their eyes into Lady Godivas spattered

with sweat and foam, aroused, they thought,
by the horses moving between our spread legs
as we clipclopped along, cross-saddle. Pictures

in newspapers christened us 'Smiling Dianas',
perfumed, still, from London ballrooms. Few knew
the other side where, the opposite of goddesses,

day in, day out, we forked out staled straw,
shirtsleeves rolled up, to the stench of ammonia
from urine, scrubbed lice and scurf

from matted coats. We prayed to saints Hippolytus,
Anne, Elgius that we might blue the mounts' blood
to stay racing on our own safe sprung turf.

Her body returned

*i.m. Edith Cavell, a member of the FANY whose body
was returned to Britain at the end of World War 1*

She rides our memories of her.
Bareback, she bends through trunks
that hold, in rings, the years she had.

Through the blue flax in fields,
Elysian, without risk of crossfire now,
she canters, sequined and plumed,

her noble profile turned to the south
into the space taken by cherry blossom
wind-woven, gold limned. All the horses

ever hers: greys, skewbalds, bays
and roans, even those she drew on walls,
pages, come to the call of her voice

echoing gently to another call:
of the first cuckoo that keeps us here
The wings she gave them, they give back

to her. While we scatter her ashes,
and the ground gives under the green
badged by primroses, they graze,

heads down, sure she will feed them still
without bowls in mud, drought and storm.
A carthorse in blinkers whickers

to the little girl she was who sat
backwards on his quarters. She can be
in every age at once: a horse goddess –

Epona, Macha – hair unplaited,
eyes shining where she dismounts,
a war heroine, to grace our hearts.

Sailor Boy

Battle of Jutland 1916

To my father

i

'One day you'll say your dear old dad
Did this and that' you'd repeat
While we protested, insisting you be
Always here – as here you are
Receding beyond the time we had.
In records of flotillas, fleets
We claim you again from history –
All the nice girls love a tar...
A sailor boy, proud in your uniform,
Proud to run away for adventure,
And wave the sceptre of Neptune,
Challenge pirates in cutlass storms,
Discover earth's every shore,
Reading tides by suns, stars, moons.

ii

Too clever for school you quit
At fourteen, auditioned in London
For a Music Hall turn, then, foaming
Into a mirror your first proper shave,
Hogs-hair brush angled into a bowsprit,
You sang out loud: *A life, a life on
The ocean wave,* already combing
Dates of birth in a mermaid's cave.
Three ages you had but fifteen you were
I think in the Battle of Jutland. Upside down,
Downside up, you swilled decks, pinching
Your nose at mates vomiting over
The rail in the swell, acting the clown
As you juggled with life-saving rings.

Not a single photograph. Wishing
I had listened more carefully, I pull,
From fathoms, syllables of your stories
Heard at bath and bedtimes, at fires
Like flares in the Skagerrak illumining
The speaking timbers in your say, the lull
Loud in your voice at losses and victories.
In the top class 'Pat the inquirer'
You'd been called. And so you learnt
And learnt, shoved in with peg-boys
Who tried to corrupt, and powder-boys
Filling magazines for rounds, burnt
By the cold. In the waves, ships like toys
You counted to the stokehold's noise.

HMS King George V – and you
A boy seaman first class, artful at dodging
Bilge rats broadside, shimmying
Up the masts, your blue eyes in rivalry
With other sight-setters, more than a few
Spiked by shards of steel. Living
With danger – still a shock to register
The quick-slow moans of casualties.
The salutes to the Admiral of side-boys
You copied as you watched the unsinkable sink,
Breaths intaken by the ship's full company
When pigeons were sent back as decoys,
German submarines like sharks slinked.
The breakers heaved, shook and shelled.

Maybe you glimpsed the sole survivor
On HMS Chester, a young gun-setter
Standing to attention, wounded, awaiting
Orders, at the slaughter on deck his fixed stare –
In heart of hearts, everyone a pacifist in war.
My father, why can I not find your letter
Tapped out on a typewriter stating
Although enemy Dreadnoughts superior,
Yours the golden fleece in every hemisphere.
To that far off boy of our blood – at the top
Of a flagpole, hoisting Jacob's ladders,
Ditty bags, then skylarking with your peers,
Hand above your eyes like the peak of the cap
Of the officer you became – three cheers.

Honorable Discharge, 1916

J E McCarthy DSCF0367

I remember him:
the limp and the stick
to support the limb
shattered irreversibly
after he had lain
for dead in Noman's land.

He never spoke
of what he had undergone;
would simply smile and joke
about his leg in the iron
that he had to lift
like a dead weight

under the piano
when he settled himself
on the stool. His fingers O
so quickly danced
as he played Chopin:
mazurkas, walzes, Polonaises.

A permanent slight shake
made his head nod
like a metronome, earth quake
in the trenches landsliding
still in his head, the repertoire
in its entirety self-taught.

I never knew him as the J E
that the photographs show,
on both legs in the army,
a handsome blond lad;
then the military hospital ward –
two long years with no bitterness –

and later his German wife
turning his sheet music on time,
tapping her feet to the life
they shared, first aid forever
in the floral lap of her frock.
Uncle Bob. His piano rippled

through me as I progressed
on the keys from 'chopsticks',
wanting him to be impressed –
and to see me walk, for him,
the secret byways he put into a book
transposed from paths of melody.

J E McCarthy: one of many
who served with honour, disabled
in the Great War, honourably
discharged 28th December, 1916:
the crumpled certificate
all that remains of him in history.

Most of the men had never seen the sea before

Wounded Punjabis in the Royal Pavilion, Brighton,

They saw it like a region more placeless than a desert,
as the sum of all their voids, a giant's tablet of glass
laid down for some prophet to write his tenets upon.

They saw it as a hydra-headed monster, its alien bellow
shattering the glass that their horses had tried to gallop over
to drink their fill, tied up forever on the horizon's taut line.

They suspected its impurity; would have prayed to the sun
to boil it before siphoning it down rays into oasis
after oasis, into each camel's bloodstream to donate

mileage without thirst for more than the usual seven days.
No help in being told it was a reservoir for all the monsoons
that had ever been; a marvel of a millpond that would drip

back to the Punjab, turning everything green. That the patterns
on its surface were those of a Persian carpet for their feet:
roses, ovals, borders woven by the light crisscrossing each face.

In panic, they turned, a wave of men about to lap inland,
away from its hump and sway backs, hands raised in minarets
for it to run out of itself, never confronted again.

Wounded Indians

Royal Pavilion, Brighton 1914–16

They thought they were dreaming
or in some kind of nirvana, transported
to a palace of domes, towers, minarets –

in another Orient, under the highest ceilings
chandelier-lit, on the walls chinoiserie,
their bed linen laundered then starched daily,

nubile white nurses washing them, tending
with their hands' ivory fans. Menus of their taste
to order, according to religion and caste,

separate utensils and kitchens. They thought
they were dreaming – in a familiar village,
but with music rooms, galleries with gilt edges,

banqueting halls, apartments for courts
of the visiting kings they had become; floors
swept of soiled dressings, an untouchable's chore.

Worth having wounds – except for the escorts
they were chained to when venturing outside.
And the seine from which they wanted to hide –

hostile, flaccid, its salt bleaching their skins
with what resembled leprous spots as it encroached
on recovery. Officially photographed,

they had no choice in the Empire's tradition
of tricking possible recruits how their compatriots,
wounded, were treated this well. In wait:

the Kitchener hospital down the road, for Indians –
dirty, without dignity, black male stewards instead
of white nurses – to which they were transferred.

Never Without You

Eleanor Farjeon to Edward Thomas, 1915

'I might meet you in London in three days'.
                    Edward Thomas to Eleanor Farjeon

Upon your return, I shall meet you in a tea shop
full of old ladies in crushed floral dresses,
beside a tiny window nailed shut against fields
harvested to smooth golds stretching beyond sight.

I shall talk merely of the heavy varnish on the beams
that I would strip to a honey colour; of the pros
and cons of Indian tea, Fry's cocoa, while we mop
our faces with starched napkins in the heat.

You will feel at ease at my not spooning,
into your cup, any joint futures. We will munch
together our toasted teacakes spread sparingly
with butter and jam. And consider each other

in the relative silence of the moment. I won't admit
I am treating us both on the proceeds of poems
pawned for having thrown themselves too whole-heartedly
at you; nor mention how the sweet peas needed picking

constantly lest they lost their scented heads; how
I have been studying the blankness of tree-poppy petals.
When I ask for more hot water, with just a splash of milk,
you will not suspect I inveigled the wind, in your absence,

to raffle to ants any wild endearments. Our eyes
will admit friendship only in their pure corners,
closing off with flaking shutters those magnetisms
hinged dangerously to the skin of the soul. I shall be

brimming to tell you how the swifts – not here
much longer – have screamed for you between houses;
how I have spoken to you like a mad thing. But instead
I shall ask for the bill. As you rummage for a tip

in your trouser pocket, clinking the loose change,
I shall keep my secret about the swallows in my rafters
making a nest out of your name. We will not need tealeaves
for predictions when we stand up to go our separate ways.

For I know the swallows, too, have other winter lives
fine as bone china to go back to. Yet their faithful revisits
year after winged year to the land I spread out
like a tablecloth will mean I am never without you.

Mourning Orders

Wm. Barker
215, 217, 219, 221 Borough High Street,
London S. E.
     Advertised in *The Lady,* 6th August, 1914, 3d

Inch by inch, slow, they slide
along the High Street in a queue
as if for rations of whelks, brawn,
their threadbare clothes dyed
in frugal attempts to look new.

Their bowed heads and silence
imply no interest in victuals.
One by one, they enter the House
Of Mourning for the armaments
of Grief, sizes large and small –

chalk and tape-measures ready,
each urgent order, as advertised,
dealt with at once. Out they file:
black figures blackened already
by smog, grime, every demise

in widows' weeds, dear-paid.
Daily they line up, hollowed eyes,
in a cortège, after saining rituals
on Borough High Street, an aubade
perhaps to overlay war-cries.

Pigeon Fancier

*'The public are reminded that homing pigeons are
doing valuable work for the government, and
are requested to assist in the suppression of
shooting of these birds. £5 reward.'*
                    Defence of the Realm

i

They flew through his dreams at night,
testing each other on high altitudes and speed,
swirling dawn suns around the pupils
of their eyes: a green, blue, purplish swoop

bred in lofts hand-carved, nailed tight
onto an aviary shrouded in moss, bindweed.
He released them daily from cliffs and hills
in practice for rescue missions of the troops.

Hard to let go of these navigators
of the magnetic fields in his own psyche,
its wreck-filled seas and head winds,

the iron particles on their beaks better
than any compass for his bearings. In alleys
of his heart they massed, to its beats underpinned.

ii

At times he let them perch on his shoulder,
called them his *love birds*, his *beaux*.
They cocked their heads at his attention,
his polishing of their bibs a rite.

In their port-wine-stained feathers
no hint that they could read prose,
letter by letter, memorise. Superior to man,
they could detect ultra violet light,

be trained to press a button in a plane
when spotting a vest on a raft in an ocean swell.
While horizons jittered from the ingredient

of their excrement in gunpowder explosions,
they cooed and strutted to the ding of a bell
at their postal deliveries – proud, he could tell.

Cher Ami, The Mocker, G.I. Joe – he said
were in the genes of every thumb feather,
heart-saddle, cere of his warrior brood:
Realm saviours who could see ten miles

or more, even in fog, their blood ruby-red
from lettings in Baghdad, by Sultans, whether
holed-up in mosques, minarets – or wooed
by Kings. Their messages he kept in a file

on tracing papers. Though gashed, shot,
in cross fire, losing eyes and feet, they made it
home to be honoured with captains' ranks.

Peion, Quishte, Culver, Cushat, Cuscote...
He calls them now by generic names as they flit,
ringed forever, from bellies of planes and tanks.

A Cloak of Birdfeathers

Susan Owen on Armistice Day

i.m. Wilfred Owen 18 March, 1893 – 4 November, 1918

i

Telegram pushed aside, willing
It to be untrue, she made her way
Through the Square to the Church.
Its spire had pierced the ground,
Sandstone walls upended, the wing
Of a carved angel, a casualty, lay
On a path. She began to search
For his name. Round and around
She walked, knowing it could never
Be mossed on a gravestone here for her
To tend. Her fingers, ink-stained
From hundreds of exchanged letters,
Penned his name on the sky's paper
Where in all his ages he remained.

ii

In the light's brittle edge, her eyes
Looked through his – at soldiers
Stepping out of cab-horses suddenly
Made of wood, himself a survivor
Of the siege of Troy, in disguise.
Yet in a crossing much nearer:
Of the Sambre-Oise canal, his identity
Shrunk to a disc, the end of war
One week away. As if in the troops,
Semi-conscious, hallucinating,
Shell-shocked like him, she heard crows
Mob above her, their black loops
Flaunting his honour, undertaking –
Their requiems hoarse, subsung below.

Armistice Day. Crazed carillons
Were wails for those killed in action,
Crying his outcry, played-out his part.
Inhaling cigarette smoke from the last den
With his mates, gas from a machine gun –
She struck matches for a conflagration,
At his request, of the closeted in his heart,
Papers on hero-worship, erotica, tokens
From dances on duck-boards he had no wish
To be remembered by. Her resort: to make him
An Icon a foot taller than he was, a believer
Depite his doubts. When the crows in a cloud
Dropped their cloak of birdfeathers
For him, he was confirmed: a Bard.

Helen Thomas visits Ivor Gurney
in the City of London Mental Asylum 1932

i

Dear Ivor, no wonder you are elsewhere
Than here, the park outside a parody
Of your rolling Cotswold hills, its benches
Scratched by jingles, at odds with your poetry.

Not a hint of a wild orchid, spiked rampion
In its flowerbeds, its fountains spat out
By stone cherubs hardly reminiscent
Of the waterfalls you loved that spout,

In dells. Dear Ivor, fifteen years back
Is an equally difficult place to be
As a private in the 2nd/5th Gloucesters,

Letters, a gas mask in your back pack.
You thrived on strict routines of rosters,
Reprieved by a special camaraderie.

ii

The corridor along which the nurses pace
Is a trench, you say, your dressing gown
A uniform, khaki, holed by shells.
Still on The Front in your head, you call

For mates long lost. The slippers you unlace
And lace are boots cracked, sucked down
In mud. You jump at the clocktower bell
As if for a whistle-blown Charge, then fall,

Colour-blinded, numbered, back into a bed
Stretcher-narrow. Post traumatic shock,
They claim. But I know different. Sane

In your insanity, you write nonstop, wed
To lines shaped as loves lost that flock
In dreams, wings, hard-won refrains.

iii

You ask me to help polish the buttons
On your pyjamas, turn bone into brass
Until you can see again your pygmy self
Distorted, ego-less in their shine.

With the cuffs of my hand-knitted cardigan
I buff away, aware this fad will pass.
Your real life breathes in books on the shelf,
Caught in your tuning fork's every tine.

Then you get me to sing along with you:
Not your own songs, just wartime snatches –
Horsey keep your tail up... Mademoiselle

From Armentières, inkypinky parlez-vous.
Naming shadows in sunlit patches,
I become your accomplice, back to the wall.

iv

Bolt-action rifles at the ready, we point
At the air while the other patients file by
In a salute. Of a sudden you order me:
'Grab him. Grab your husband from death.

He does not want a priest to anoint
His brow, but to see again a sky
Skud over watermeadows, pick a posy
For your vase, then to swap on his breath –

For choruses every dawn – old army gongs.
In solitude he collects the midnight rain
With which to christen you as you were

Before bereavement. Too long, too long:
A decade and a half. For you in haunted lanes
He grows Honesty, ransoms, larkspur.'

Dear Ivor, as you clench your fists, twitch
And mutter, I see the tailors in your blood
Stitching this cold confined space,
Its barred windows you have withstood

Year after year – with fields. Each bank and ditch
That wild flowers, weeds, mosses stud,
Each byway, stile – you search for a trace
Of yourself and Edward exploring hill, wood.

And then I bring you his old ordnance maps
Creased, cracked, stained – but O what joy.
Your fingers march along unmarked tracks

Tracing companionship despite your memory-lapse.
Prayers for death no more. You smile like a boy,
Shake and shake my hand: your life back.

Too soon, Ivor, walks re-taken, conversations
Revised, you distance yourself from me,
Not so far as Edward since you stay here,
Still, in your tall, gaunt body, your stare

Intense as a blowlamp, deep in visions.
They are getting at you through the frequency
Of the wireless, you claim, are near –
Unpicking with their nails the locks on doors.

In the Common Room where you slouch,
Jaw hanging, with the other inmates,
I sit at the piano, begin to play: *Fur Elise*

Before you the musician to whom I vouched
My fingers worked no more. If a chord is late,
Notes wrong, I continue – for your heart's ease.

Eleanor Farjeon's Death, 1965

Helen Thomas speaks

i

Like losing a daughter: the day you died.
I remembered the silliest details:
You peeling potatoes into a bucket
Without water, cooking only potatoes,

Earth-powdered, for dinner, trying to hide –
When his love for me had grown stale –
The blush on your fresh face at the sight
Of him waving beneath the window.

In the library you sat, determined to learn
The names of all the flowers he knew,
The birdsong he would test you on with just

A brush of lips between you. When ravens
Blackened into his demons that flew
Through me, glad was I of you in our midst.

ii

Like losing a friend: the day you died –
Who held me when he fell on a foreign field,
Whose letters and parcels to him on the Front
Lightened his marching foot's stride,

His game dodging shells, danger denied.
For house martins, owls his eyes were peeled
As if on home ground – still on a hunt
For sightings rare, your smile by his side.

My revelations in prose hard to forgive
You plucked from his poems overlaid
With their pall, then typed them anew.

I envy how you managed to outlive
The legend he was, ensuring that he stayed
True to a code for your obsession to pursue.

iii

The unattainable he fell in love with, with you.
Your naiveté charmed him, your devotion
Doubled mine. But every domestic duty
I did for him scrubbed me out of his dream.

Behind your spectacles did you see me renew
My martyrdom, pray for those love potions:
The youth of one woman, the beauty
Of another, leaked from his eyes' sharp gleam?

Did you ever think to tell me his long walks
Were specially planned escapes from our home
Where I got on his nerves, his pretext a wish

For new nature notes? And what of the talks
Not shared with me? For you both, silent tomes
To browse now behind the curtain's last swish.

iv

What would he have thought of me today:
Lines scribbled on my forehead, crowsfeet
Crinkling my eyes, hidden away from life,
Cut off by joint friends, many of them gone?

He appears, at times, in the sun as it xrays
Moving shadows – stops to greet
My shrivelled form, never surely his wife.
Preserved in his prime as an icon

I did not want him distorted, canonised
By decease. Nor just for therapy did I write –
But to keep him imperfect, real, our stories

Breathing, intact. Though criticised
For betrayal, his loss I could not fight
Without frankness. Eleanor, grant me peace.

Stone Cottage

*Yeats and Pound in Ashdown Forest, Sussex
during The Great War*

i

Blue-blooded words they wanted,
An exclusive brotherhood moving in,
Ravens on ridge tiles, mewing buzzards
Bossing the ether higher than ever before.
Up chimney flues they blew to be haunted
By bodies in souls, by a wild spin
Of golden leaves the beech trees shed
Into gowns which their muses wore.
Three winters long they centred
Themselves behind a warped oak door
Scratched by gales that riddled their minds,
Leaves, twigs, rushes woven into blinds
For windows to keep out 'the wild moor' –
Lyrics, texturing walls, counter-signed.

ii

Three winters long in the fall of dark
The young poet read, to the elder, songs –
Conjuring, for visions, a stone-crop past,
Stag-hunters reining in on King's Standing,
Breath of bones under the heath's firm chalk –
The war at a remove far as Sparta among
Birches and pines bent by seasonal blasts.
Yet in its persistence, both poets felt the sting
From casualties they knew. As boots trudged
Down the Roman Road, forest rides,
Coleman's Hatch, Wych Cross, Duddleswell:
Regiments on manoeuvres, soles wedged
With mud, their words began to take up sides –
On retreat no longer, explosive as shells.

iii

An American unable to enlist, Pound
Stepped proud into the tested uniform of Li Po,
Translating lines genuine enough to be
That person on The Front where souls in bodies
Fought in sagas from around
The world, all wars at once in the throw
Of a dice by Time's fey geometries.
Mess-tins, sandbags had his energy –
With Yeats, too, hurt into utterance
By the cheated dead and their dead gods.
Three winters long lit by the lamp of new lines
From pens dipped in loam, crossed like swords,
'the wild moor' staged its own scrub clearance –
Dreaming backwards through lark-seared chines.

Last Letter

Katharine Tynan to Francis Ledwidge
after his death, 31 July 1917 in the battle of Passchendaele

A last letter I write on the backs
of places you were homesick for:
Crewbawn, Crocknaharna, Currabwee

while you laid a road for an assault,
or in a mud hole crouched drinking tea.
From a different Front, your words to me

form raindrop-rosaries on cobwebs
read by the sun between the fence posts
you scribbled upon, their chants blown

by the winds you gentle – over the hill
of Slane. I recall death a challenge
great as life to you, its secret under stones

of those passage-tombs of Knowth,
Newgrange, Dowth you tapped, fingers
playing the river Boyne's flecked fluency,

Tell me, Francis, what is the banishment –
murmured by Meister Eckhart, wished for
in wells – of an alone-ness tough as the winter

you endured, rheumatic in the Balkans,
on your trudge to Salonika? Hung up
with your boots: your mortal coil. A lorica

I send you. Like the legendary witch, let me
drop a cairn for you to remain here in the spell
of Crewbawn, Crocknaharna, Currabwee.

Virginia Woolf's Angels 1919

'Whenever I felt the shadow of her wing or the radiance
of her halo upon my page, I took up the inkpot and flung it at her.
She died hard.'
      Virginia Woolf of 'The Angel in the House' by Coventry Patmore.

Five years after their rescue
Of troops beaten back in Mons,
She danced with them on the downs,
Their forms like kites she reeled in
With clouds, their haloes askew
On waves of green escarpments
Breaking into the sea. Beech-brown
The combes she looked down upon
While the angels held up her skirts,
Rode the rhythms of her walking feet –
Their wings no longer torn.
In a host they balanced, on the alert
For ancient armies in retreat
Squatting in hunched hawthorns.

One year after the armistice
In the steep slopes of her temperament
She kept them at her side, to banish
The simpering angels of the house
At whom, with the sedge, they would hiss.
Whenever an alien shadow bent
Over her page as she wrote, a swish
Of wings dipped in ink would douse
Its creeping insistence, despatch it
Into tumuli turfed over, into dew ponds.
The angels of Mons were her guides
Through plankton, fossils, flint; could fit
Into her psyche's darkest corners beyond
Precipices chalked in over sucking tides.

Recuperation 1919

Ford Madox Ford in Hurston, Pulborough, Sussex

At Hurston, he withdrew to the land;
Tried not to think of it as fertilised
By the bones of his mates when he curved
Corrugated iron into arks for the pigs
He bought with a nod and raised hand
At market. In the rented cottage he devised
Traps for rats that slithered and swerved
Under his feet. While he poked them with twigs,
They jumped for the light over his shoulders,
Worlds of war and books obscured
In the swill his lover mixed, her shawl
A plug for draughts, ghosts of elders
Tapping the plaster and lath, immured.

Tamworths, Saddlebacks, Berkshires...
Their intelligence, mud-sucked, higher
Than many generals on the Western Front,
Their power to predict the wind
Before it arrived better than a wetted finger.
He was Odysseus wandering through byres
And sties to a fanfare of snouts, squeals, grunts –
As, a swine-herd, he tried to find
His regenerated self stolen with his name
By a shell at the Somme, Ypres-Salient.
He stroked the devouring pigs as they died
Farrowing, or from flu, felt no shame
When the blood from the litter they ate went
Into his veins, donated to the maimed, purified.

Horse Worshipper

Franz Marc, 1880-1916

He had always worshipped them:
at grass, nuzzling each other's manes,
their suspended, extravagant paces

when spooked by a brace of pheasants,
by stags leaping out of the woods.
Their Roman noses, dished faces

he studied, matching their instinct
of flight and fear with his own.
The language of a snort, whinny,

ears forward, back, he translated
into human speech as he looked through
their eyes, a seer, yet unable to see

forwards now, strong in backward
and side vision. Stallions, mares, geldings
lemon and blue he bred from brushes –

their conformation soft-curved
in layers of human flesh. Shape-changing,
he rode out of farms and villages

in France, cornfields squirled
by the wind compared with Van Gogh's.
In the violet shadows of war

he wished to convert the panic, pain –
all his – of horses back into abstracts
broken, fighting, playing, to restore

their heroic forms in a studio back home.
There, battle, no longer the purification
once seemed, could be unlearnt.

Yet he was out there, in his kitbag
the Gospel of St. Mark, splashes scribbled
in ink in sketchpads. *Briefe aus dem Feld:*

his last indelible words of joy, about to be
discharged, on his wife's heart. Sudden –
that day, a shell killed him in Verdun.

Tower of Blue Horses

Franz Marc, 1913

How well, with the horses
in his veins, he let them
construct from their own forms
an eternal blue tower. Still
yet moving, they slid downhill
to a halt, nose to tail, ears
pricked, heads to the left, alert,
terror in the allseeing eye
of the lead horse, those behind
wild-eyed, bloodshot, blind.
How well he knew them –
different from the ridden horses
of the apocalypse: of conquest,
war, famine, death – red, white,
blacker than the darkest night.
These that came to the call
of his brushes were riderless,
drained of colour, solid
yet transparent – cut from
the glass that shattered them.
How well he knew this herd
life-size, of reflection, of dream,
shod in the sad sounds of blue,
their bucking off of enmities,
the anatomy of their geometries.
Frame outgrown, they stand
in a future already their past,
arched over by a rainbow stained
orange from dried blood, scars
slithers now of moons and stars.
With rumps for the central column,
their bellies the sides, the tower
leans with them, never to topple:
a memorial to each hoof, bone, sinew.
How well, very well he knew.

Lady of the Black Horse

Mabel St Clair Stobart, 1862-1954

(oil on canvas, by George James Rankin, 1916)

Lady of our worst fears,
you ride over the precipices of our hearts,
looking through your black horse's ears
beyond, always beyond the self
whose jesters and fools play amateur parts
in the drama of a life's limited years.

Lady of ladies, in a frame,
an ideal the brush strokes idealise.
Our of care for those whose cause you claim,
behind the canvas, a medical convoy
you train, crowsfeet at your eyes,
through bog myrtle, bramble, broom.

Lady of Studland's longest sands,
of the fuchsia bells' tolls over the ling.
In a major's uniform you give commands
to forget the fear that fractures wings,
to duck down at top speed through alders,
up dunes, on slippery seaweed strands.

Lady of the Serbian retreat,
of field camps behind a front line, aiding
refugees to carry their breaths as you beat
back typhus, rig up dressing stations.
Onto leaden skies most of them cling –
hobnailed by blisters frozen onto their feet.

Lady of tightrope tracks,
of last and first moments, you emerge
elegant, an army intact, from the marathon trek –
no loss of personnel – through ranges
of needles snow-coated, corpse-lined gorges,
a shelter in the odd monastery or shack.

Lady of the blackest horse,
while seahorses snort – and grebes, warblers,
divers start up from Dorset's scrub and gorse,
we search in the marram grass for wagons
rolling on spiders' threads, listen for your orders.
Salt winds beyond the bay have your force.

Sewing Patterns

(for Nana, 1885-1970)

For years, the Singer sewing machine stood
in the corner of the room, an unused curiosity,
indoor plants climbing around the iron lattices
of its frame; a photograph on its surface
of a grandfather never known in army uniform.

Its treadle bore faint imprints of dancing feet,
one in front of the other, following the wheel.
To and fro, to and fro – the front room walls
swayed to the rhythm. I pictured my grandmother
letting her child choose the threads

for bobbins, then, fingers beware, winding them
through riddles of loops and hooks. Her habit
to suck the thread before aiming it, eyes strained,
head at a tilt, through the elusive slit of the needle.
And them both fiddling with another thread

before pulling it, from a sliding silver lid,
into a cat's cradle. Many performed
these rituals, my grandmother recalled, saving up
patterns: *Vogue, Simplicity, Butterick, McCall*
to transform lengths of twill gabardine

into waterproof clothes for the troops. Nothing
was too ambitious: trench-coats, breeches
begun as tissue-paper shapes perforated with dots.
Pins in pursed lips, they would iron them
with their palms, then hold them to the light

like skins already shed, or ghosts that could make
no peace with death. Such a task to sew them up,
fit them back tight onto an exposed body in need
of a carapace. I can hear my grandmother now,
though long gone, treadling the treadle

idle in the corner while, steadily, I guide
her memories on the sewing machine through dust –
lock, chain, zigzag stitches in the straightest lines
her legacy for wounds. Empty now the drawer
for bobbins that spun with such industry.

Bell Ringers

April 1914, St. Dunstan's Church, Mayfield

Arthur Groombridge, John Thurlow, Basil Paine –
each of your bells polished by your pride
in the ringing chamber where you swung

from ropes as if from trees in Park Wood.
Every pull sent storms away from the ridge
to rumble around the valley, *striking*

your expertise. You are heard there still: splicing
bell ropes, muttering numbers and names
Minimus, Minor, Major, Royal, Maximus…

Singles, Doubles, Triples, Caters, Cinques…
miniature thunder gods reciting what teachers
never taught, patterns and rows in beats

steady as the clop of horses along the High Street,
steady as your fit young hearts, the sap
in your veins that month from bluebell woods,

primroses and drifting blossom on your breath.
You should have stayed where wild orchids grew
at your feet, doing cartwheel call-changes,

calling up, calling down, swapping bells
in a Mayfield of mayweed, maypoles, maids. But –
escaping from St. Dunstan's tongs, a devilish clash

of shellfire in your ears silenced all bells.
How much better for you to have been killed
holding onto wet ropes in a local thunderstorm

while ringing that half peal of Grandsire Triples
to celebrate the new village school. Each clapper,
muffled fully now, evokes you with its elegies.

Notes

The change from sidesaddle to cross-saddle, or riding astride, was regarded by many males as indecent. It was (wrongly) thought that women gained sexual satisfaction riding astride and were lewd, bawdy creatures.

Page 52:
Mabel St Clair Stobart 1862 – 1954, was born in Hurst Green, East Sussex but lived for many years in Dorset. A supporter of the suffragette movement before the First World War, she was a member of the FANY (First Aid Nursing Yeomanry). Then she founded the Women's Sick and Wounded Convoy Corps (1912) and the Women's National Service League (1914). She served, as well as in Belgium, on the Balkan Front where, a major, in her fifties, she commanded the Serbian Relief Fund's Front Line Field Hospital. She and her medical staff accompanied the Serbian Army's retreat through the Albanian mountains.